LANDMARKS IN MY COMMUNITY

THE FIREHOUSE

FIRE DEPT.

BY SADIE SILVA

Gareth Stevens
PUBLISHING

Please visit our website, www.garethstevens.com. For a free color catalog of all our high-quality books, call toll free 1-800-542-2595 or fax 1-877-542-2596.

Library of Congress Cataloging-in-Publication Data
Names: Silva, Sadie, author.
Title: The firehouse / Sadie Silva.
Description: Buffalo, NY : Gareth Stevens, [2025] | Series: Landmarks in my community | Includes bibliographical references and index.
Identifiers: LCCN 2023034820 (print) | LCCN 2023034821 (ebook) | ISBN 9781538293102 (library binding) | ISBN 9781538293096 (paperback) | ISBN 9781538293119 (ebook)
Subjects: LCSH: Fire stations–Juvenile literature. | Fire extinction–Juvenile literature. | Fire fighters–Juvenile literature.
Classification: LCC TH9148 .S5345 2025 (print) | LCC TH9148 (ebook) | DDC 363.37–dc23/eng/20230821
LC record available at https://lccn.loc.gov/2023034820
LC ebook record available at https://lccn.loc.gov/2023034821

Published in 2025 by
Gareth Stevens Publishing
2544 Clinton Street
Buffalo, NY 14224

Designer: Andrea Davison-Bartolotta
Editor: Caitie McAneney

Photo credits: Cover, p. 1 AlexSava/iStockphoto.com; series art (page numbers) art_of_sun/Shutterstock.com; series art (map background) Marian Salabai/Shutterstock.com; p. 5 Wileydoc/Shutterstock.com; p. 7 BrianEKushner/iStockphoto.com; p. 9 prochasson frederic/Shutterstock.com; p. 11 marge wolfe/Shutterstock.com; pp. 13, 17 Monkey Business Images/Shutterstock.com; p. 15 Evgenia Parajanian/Shutterstock.com; p. 19 Frame Stock Footage/Shutterstock.com; p. 21 Tyler Olson/Shutterstock.com.

Printed in the United States of America

Some of the images in this book illustrate individuals who are models. The depictions do not imply actual situations or events.

CPSIA compliance information: Batch #CS25GS: For further information contact Gareth Stevens, New York, New York at 1-800-542-2595.

Find us on

CONTENTS

Boldface words appear in the glossary.

A Visit to the Firehouse

Have you ever visited a firehouse? It's an important part of any community. It's where firefighters wait for calls to put out a fire. It's also where important **equipment** is kept, such as hoses and fire trucks.

At the Firehouse

A firehouse is often a large building. It has a large space for storing fire trucks and equipment. Some firehouses have offices and places for firefighters to sleep. Firefighters may wait at the firehouse until they get a call.

Exciting Equipment

Everything firefighters need is at the firehouse. They have big fire trucks, which often have ladders on them. They also have hoses for spraying water on flames. They may also have **fire extinguishers**.

8

Dressed for Safety

The firehouse also has all the clothes and gear that firefighters need. They keep firefighters safe from flames, smoke, and heat. Their special clothes cannot catch fire. Many wear a helmet and a mask that gives them fresh air.

A Firefighter's Job

Some communities have **professional** firefighters. They stay at the firehouse in **shifts**. When a call comes, they rush to the **scene**! Smaller communities may have firefighters who are mostly **volunteers** or work fewer hours.

Firefighters help put out fires. They also teach people about fire safety! They go to schools to talk to kids about staying safe. Sometimes, they let kids visit the firehouse to see the equipment and building up close.

Keeping the Community Safe

Firehouses are needed in a community. They keep the community safe from harmful fires. People can call 911 when they have a fire. Then, firefighters can grab their gear from the firehouse and save the day!

Firefighters also leave the firehouse to help with other **emergencies**. They go to the scene of car crashes. They may be called to help people who are hurt or having a **medical** emergency too.

Your Community Firehouse

Where is your community firehouse? Some communities have more than one. You can ask your parents where it is. You can ask your teacher if a firefighter can visit your class. Fire safety is important for all communities!

20

GLOSSARY

emergency: A problem that needs quick action.

equipment: Tools, clothing, and other items needed for a job.

fire extinguisher: A tool with chemicals in it used to spray fire and put it out.

medical: Having to do with care given to people who are sick or hurt.

professional: Having to do with a job someone does for a living.

scene: Where something happened.

shift: A regular time period when people work.

volunteer: To work without pay.

FOR MORE INFORMATION

BOOKS

Anderson, AnnMarie. *Meet a Firefighter!* New York, NY: Children's Press, 2021.

Minden, Cecilia. *Firefighters.* Parker, CO: Wonder Books, 2023.

WEBSITES

Fire Station Facts for Kids
kids.kiddle.co/Fire_station
Learn more about all that goes on at a firehouse!

Firefighter
kids.britannica.com/kids/article/firefighter/624512
Do you want to be a firefighter? Learn more about the job!

INDEX